Persevërance

MARIE LAZZARA

BOOK SERIES BY FIG FACTOR MEDIA

WordPower Book Series

© Copyright 2021, Fig Factor Media, LLC.
All rights reserved.

All rights reserved. No portion of this book may be reproduced by mechanical, photographic or electronic process, nor may it be stored in a retrieval system, transmitted in any form or otherwise be copied for public use or private use without written permission of the copyright owner.

It is sold with the understanding that the publisher and the individual authors are not engaged in the rendering of psychological, legal, accounting or other professional advice. The content and views in each chapter are the sole expression and opinion of its author and not necessarily the views of Fig Factor Media, LLC.

For more information, contact:

Fig Factor Media, LLC | www.figfactormedia.com

Cover Design & Layout by Juan Pablo Ruiz
Printed in the United States of America

ISBN: 978-1-957058-02-3
Library of Congress Control Number: 2021923677

DEDICATION

I dedicate this book to my devoted and loving husband of 23 years, Loreto Vito Lazzara, our two beautiful children, David and Alessandra, my parents, Marco and Sharon Piscitelli, and my brother, James Piscitelli.

ACKNOWLEDGMENTS

I would like to thank my friend and boss Jacqueline S. Ruiz for offering me and others this special opportunity to be an author. I'm also thanking my supportive JJR marketing co-workers Kylie Knur and Gaby Hernandez Franch; Sensei Josh Weiser and my fellow aikido practitioners at North Shore Aikido, LLC; Bill Wilder who leads our great choirs at St. Philip the Apostle Catholic Church in Addison, and my voice teacher Michelle Maiers for always encouraging me to be the best and to never give up. I also want to thank my closest friends who have been constant sources of strength in my life: Carmela Sclafani, Cheryl Price, and my mentor Rose Marie Mikoljak. Lastly, I thank almighty God and Jesus Christ for the gifts of the written word and the uplifted voice.

INTRO

I chose the word perseverance because it has been an innate part of my personality. The Merriam-Webster dictionary defines perseverance as the "continued effort to do or achieve something despite difficulties, failure, or opposition." To me, it has always meant to never give up, no matter how hard the circumstances are. My husband Vito jokes that, "If you're not six feet under, then it's a good day." He's right—if you're not dead, you're living. Whether that is in good or bad circumstances, it is something to celebrate.

Aside from my work as Public Relations Manager with JJR Marketing, I also cantor (sing) at funeral Masses at my Catholic church. Funerals remind me of my own mortality. When God calls you home, you can't say no. The time to explore your world and to make differences in your life and others' lives is now.

Death, metaphorically speaking, "kills" perseverance, curiosity, and life. A closed casket or lidded urn can represent someone who doesn't want to live to the fullest, reach that insurmountable goal, or be open to possibilities. We should never close the door on something without pursuing a solution, a goal, or a passion. This is what perseverance calls us to do.

Let us not be people of the grave but people of life, willing to venture on roads no matter how rocky or hilly they are!

RECEIVING PERSEVERANCE THROUGH FAITH

New American Bible, Revised Romans 5: 1-5:

"We celebrate in hope of the glory of God. And not only this, but we also celebrate in our tribulations, knowing that tribulation brings about perseverance, proven character, hope and hope does not disappoint, because the love of God has been poured out within our hearts through the Holy Spirit who was given to us."

God has given us times to endure various trials and tribulations so that we can look back at these instances to help us become stronger and wiser people. He has a plan for everyone and supports believers with constant, unconditional love and guidance through the Holy Spirit.

USING HUMOR TO GET THROUGH THE BAD TIMES

Difficult situations such as a disagreement with a friend, a falling out with a boss or the disappointment of not reaching a goal are periods that we want to avoid at all times. Who relishes involvement in catastrophe? No one. However, if we step back, and look at the situation through a different lens we may find a little bit of levity to get us through life.

FALLING DOWN

In the Japanese martial art of aikido, we are often reminded about a powerful proverb, "Nana korobi, ya oki" which translates to "fall seven times, stand up eight." We, as aikido students, take many falls. The proverb describes how life can bring us many defeats but we need to stand tall and stand again.

HITTING THE RIGHT NOTE

Before I cantor for Masses, I practice the songs during the week so I am prepared. But one Sunday morning, I realized one song I had practiced was not the one being played. I had practiced a song with the same title but a different melody.

Surprised that I didn't practice the correct version of the song, my music director went over the hymn twice so I could get the right notes and melody in my mind. With 30 minutes to go before Mass, I felt a crashing wave of anxiety and wondered how was I going to pull this off? Summoning up my musical knowledge, I realized that there is a pattern to follow and if I can do some sight reading and master the flow, I can get through the song. That positive thought stopped my anxious feelings from paralyzing me. During Mass, I prayed hard for God to help me through the experience. He did! It also helped that my director sang with me.

Even with a scary situation, you must push through. Believe! You can persevere.

RIDING HIGH

Recently, my supervisor and friend gifted our team a beautiful trip to Puerto Vallarta. One of the trip's activities was riding an electric bike. I hadn't ridden a bicycle in over 40 years. But there I was cruising downtown Puerto Vallarta trying to avoid cars and people! I could have said no, forget it, but I decided to do it because it was a brave and new adventure that led me to persevere even in uncertain terrain. So, be open to traveling down a new path for it can lead to a new adventure.

DREAMING THE IMPOSSIBLE DREAM

One song that I enjoy is "The Impossible Dream (The Quest)" from the 1965 Broadway musical *Man of La Mancha*. In the musical, Don Quixote, an elderly nobleman, calls himself a "knight errant" and fights for good and the love of a maiden. He never gives up the fight and neither should we when the cause is just.

QUOTING SOMEONE ON PERSEVERANCE

"Perseverance is stubbornness with a purpose"—John Shipp. That describes me perfectly. I've been called stubborn before and there's a reason for it. If I have a gut feeling that something isn't right, I will question it or correct. Never settle for something if it seems good on face value; go beyond the surface.

CONNECTING WITH THE MEDIA

Public relations specialists have to think creatively when pitching across different media platforms whether it is a newspaper, television station, magazines, or a niche podcast. It takes time to make opportunities happen. Good opportunities aren't overnight successes. When the opportunity occurs, there is a win/win between clients showing expertise and publicists using time and talent to make beneficial connections with reporters, editors, and hosts.

PARENTING A CHILD ON THE AUTISM SPECTRUM

Parents, like myself, who have children on the autism spectrum have unique qualities of compassion, patience, ingenuity, and perseverance. We give it our all so that our children are treated with respect, love, understanding, and the chance to succeed in life. Parents who love their children don't sit back when obstacles get in their way. They look for solutions and get other like-minded people involved to bring about positive change so that every child no matter what their race, sex, creed or disability can thrive.

ADMIRING THE COURAGEOUS LION

The lion, to me, has always been a symbol of courage, fortitude, and perseverance. This quote by Mary Anne Radmacher captures what true courage is about: "Courage doesn't always roar. Sometimes courage is the little voice at the end of the day that says I'll try again tomorrow."

We must persist.

FINDING ANOTHER WAY IN A DIFFICULT SITUATION

We all make mistakes, and sometimes we retreat, fearing we might cause other errors. There is always another way to make things right if we have the courage to take that first step. One step leads to another and another—never give up on the right solution.

KNOCKING ON EVERY POSSIBLE DOOR

A few years after giving birth to fraternal twins, I wanted to get back into the workplace. It was rough and difficult to find a job in public relations. I interviewed people, went to job and networking workshops, and presented a podcast to find that someone who would want me to join their team. A chance meeting at a public relations get-together is how I met my current employer. You need to keep knocking until someone lets you into a new, exciting opportunity.

ABOUT THE AUTHOR

Marie Lazzara is the Public Relations Manager with JJR Marketing, Inc. in Naperville, Illinois. She oversees duties such as conducting media relations on behalf of JJR and its clients, creating media placement pitches and story development and coordinating media outlet interviews with clients. Prior to her joining JJR in 2014, Lazzara has over 17 years-experience being a feature reporter for Illinois-based news media outlets such as Shaw Media, Daily Herald, Patch and Tribune Media Group. She has a bachelor's in communications degree from Dominican University in River Forest, Illinois and a master's of journalism from Roosevelt University in Chicago. She resides in Addison, Illinois with her husband Loreto Vito Lazzara and two children David and Alessandra.

www.ingramcontent.com/pod-product-compliance
Lightning Source LLC
Chambersburg PA
CBHW041235240426

43673CB00011B/345